Bones

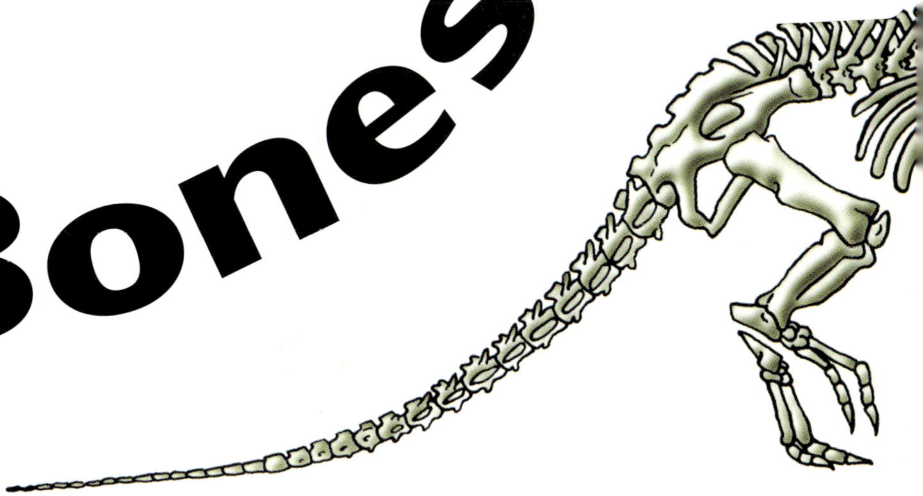

Jan Pritchett • Illustrated by Ben Spiby

Rigby

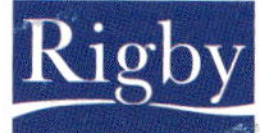

Which one has bones?

The bird has bones.

a slug

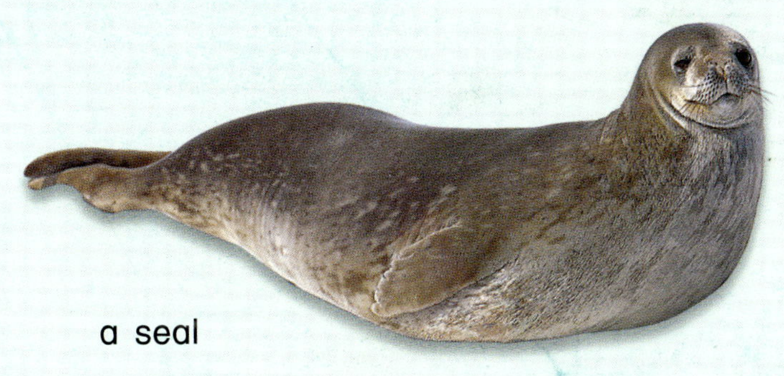

a seal

Which one has bones?

The seal has bones.

a snail

a tortoise

Which one has bones?

The tortoise has bones.

a fish

a jellyfish

Which one has bones?

The fish has bones.

Which one has bones?

The armadillo has bones.

a snake

a worm

Which one has bones?

The snake has bones.

a rhinoceros beetle

a rhinoceros

Which one has bones?

The rhinoceros has bones.